Kristen Stewart

ABDO
Publishing Company

Big Buddy BOOKS
Buddy Bios

by Sarah Tieck

VISIT US AT
www.abdopublishing.com

Published by ABDO Publishing Company, 8000 West 78th Street, Edina, Minnesota 55439.

Copyright © 2011 by Abdo Consulting Group, Inc. International copyrights reserved in all countries. No part of this book may be reproduced in any form without written permission from the publisher. Big Buddy Books™ is a trademark and logo of ABDO Publishing Company.

Printed in the United States of America, North Mankato, Minnesota.
052010
092010

 PRINTED ON RECYCLED PAPER

Coordinating Series Editor: Rochelle Baltzer
Contributing Editors: Heidi M.D. Elston, Megan M. Gunderson, BreAnn Rumsch, Marcia Zappa
Graphic Design: Maria Hosley
Cover Photograph: *AP Photo*: Sipa via AP Images.
Interior Photographs/Illustrations: *AP Photo*: Carlo Allegri (p. 29), AP Photo (p. 17), Dana Edelson/NBCU Photo Bank via AP Images (p. 17), Paul Drinkwater/NBCU Photo Bank via AP Images (p. 21), Robert E. Klein (p. 17), Chris Pizzello (p. 5), Matt Sayles (pp. 19, 24), Sipa via AP Images (p. 19); *Getty Images*: Larry Busacca (p. 11), Gregg DeGuire (p. 9), Tom Kingston (p. 13), Jason LaVeris/FilmMagic (p. 27), Todd Williamson (p. 14), Kevin Winter (p. 15); *Shutterstock*: inginsh (p. 23), Carlos A. Torres (p. 7).

Library of Congress Cataloging-in-Publication Data

Tieck, Sarah, 1976-
 Kristen Stewart : Twilight star / Sarah Tieck.
  p. cm. -- (Big buddy biographies)
 ISBN 978-1-61613-977-3
 1. Stewart, Kristen, 1990---Juvenile literature. 2. Actors--United States--Biography--Juvenile literature. I. Title.
 PN2287.S685T54 2010
 791.4302'8092--dc22
 [B]
                         2010013423

Kristen
Stewart

Contents

Kristen plays Isabella "Bella" Swan in the Twilight movies.

Rising Star

Kristen Stewart is a talented actress. She has appeared in several popular movies. Kristen is best known for starring in the Twilight movie **series**.

Oregon

Nevada

PACIFIC OCEAN

California

Arizona

Los Angeles

N W E S

MEXICO

ONE WILSHIRE

Family Ties

Kristen Jaymes Stewart was born in Los Angeles, California, on April 9, 1990. Her parents are Jules Mann-Stewart and John Stewart. Kristen has an older brother named Cameron.

Los Angeles is a large city. It is known for having many acting opportunities.

Growing Up

Kristen grew up in the Los Angeles area. Both her parents work in show business. But, they are not actors. They work behind the scenes on television shows and movies.

When she was young, Kristen learned about show business from her parents.

In elementary school, Kristen appeared in school shows. When she was eight, an **agent** saw her sing in a holiday show. The agent asked her to try out for **professional** acting parts.

Kristen told her parents she wanted to try out. At first, they were not sure she should. But, they agreed to let her.

Kristen began acting when she was very young. She grew up in front of the cameras.

Starting Out

Kristen became a professional actress in 1999. She had a few small, non-speaking roles in movies. Then in 2001, she acted in *The Safety of Objects*. This was her first big movie role!

In 2002, Kristen acted in *Panic Room*. In this movie, Kristen worked with famous actress Jodie Foster. This role helped Kristen strengthen her acting skills.

Kristen (*right*) played the daughter of Jodie Foster (*left*) in the thriller *Panic Room*.

13

A Working Actress

After *Panic Room*, people began to notice Kristen's acting talent. This helped her get more movie **roles**.

Kristen appeared in *Cold Creek Manor* in 2003 and *Catch That Kid* in 2004. In 2005, she acted in *Zathura: A Space Adventure*. Kristen starred in *The Messengers* in 2007. That same year, she had an important part in *Into the Wild*.

Kristen worked with Josh Hutcherson, Jon Favreau, Dax Shepard, and Jonah Bobo (*left to right*) on *Zathura: A Space Adventure*. The movie is about two brothers who go on a magical journey in space.

Did you know...

Emile Hirsch knows *Twilight*'s director Catherine Hardwicke. He told her that Kristen should play Bella in *Twilight*.

Music Lover

Kristen is a music fan. In her free time, she listens to music. And, Kristen can play the **guitar**.

Kristen has played musical artists in movies. In *Into the Wild*, she sang and played guitar. Kristen played electric guitar in *The Runaways*. Still, many fans don't know she can play in real life!

Kristen likes many kinds of music. Some of her favorite artists are the Beatles (*left*), Beck (*above*), and Radiohead (*right*).

Big Break

In 2008, Kristen starred in the movie *Twilight*. She played a teenager named Isabella "Bella" Swan.

Twilight is the story of Bella and a vampire named Edward Cullen. In stories, vampires are usually scary. But, Edward is nice. He watches out for Bella.

The Twilight movies are based on a popular book series by Stephenie Meyer. These books have broken sales records.

In 2009, Kristen starred in *The Twilight Saga: New Moon*. She also worked on the third movie in the **series**. *The Twilight Saga: Eclipse* came out in 2010.

The Twilight movies were very popular. *Twilight* even won awards! This success helped Kristen grow as a movie star. Now, reporters often **interview** her. And, stories and pictures of her appear in magazines and newspapers.

Kristen has been a guest on radio and television shows. In 2009, television host Conan O'Brien interviewed her.

An Actress's Life

As an actress, Kristen is very busy! She spends time practicing lines. During filming, she works on a movie set for several hours each day.

Sometimes, Kristen travels to other states or countries to make movies. She may be away from home for several months.

Movie sets contain cameras and props.
Props are objects that are used in movies.

Kristen is very well known.
Reporters often take her picture.

24

Did you know...

Kristen's acting work made it hard for her to attend school. So, she worked with private teachers to complete high school.

As an actress, Kristen also travels to attend events and meet fans. Her fans are very excited to see her. Kristen often feels shy, so this much attention can be hard.

25

Off the Screen

When Kristen isn't on **set** or traveling, she spends time at home. She enjoys hanging out with her family. She also likes to read books.

Kristen supports causes that are important to her. In 2008, she helped raise money for children with diabetes.

27

Did you know...

The Runaways is about a famous 1980s rock star named Joan Jett. Kristen got to meet the real-life Joan Jett while working on the movie.

Kristen (*left*) is friends with actress Dakota Fanning (*right*). They starred in *The Runaways* together. Kristen played rock star Joan Jett, and Dakota played singer Cherie Currie.

Buzz

Kristen's fame continues to grow. In 2010, she starred in *The Runaways*.

Kristen hopes to attend college someday. She says she would like to study **literature** and become a writer.

Fans are excited to see what's next for Kristen Stewart. Many believe she has a bright **future**!

Snapshot

★**Name**: Kristen Jaymes Stewart

★**Birthday**: April 9, 1990

★**Birthplace**: Los Angeles, California

★**Appearances**: *The Safety of Objects, Panic Room, Cold Creek Manor, Catch That Kid, Zathura: A Space Adventure, The Messengers, Into the Wild, Twilight, The Twilight Saga: New Moon, The Twilight Saga: Eclipse, The Runaways*

Important Words

agent a person who works to help actors get jobs.

future (FYOO-chuhr) a time that has not yet occurred.

guitar (guh-TAHR) a stringed musical instrument played by strumming.

interview to ask someone a series of questions.

lines the words an actor says in a play, a movie, or a show.

literature (LIH-tuh-ruh-chur) writings, such as books or poems, that have lasting artistic value.

professional (pruh-FEHSH-nuhl) working for money rather than for pleasure.

role a part an actor plays.

series a set of similar things or events in order.

set the place where a movie or a television show is recorded.

Web Sites

To learn more about Kristen Stewart, visit ABDO Publishing Company online. Web sites about Kristen Stewart are featured on our Book Links page. These links are routinely monitored and updated to provide the most current information available.

www.abdopublishing.com

Index